At the Hospital

Written by Roderick Hunt and Annemarie Young

Illustrated by Alex Brychta

OXFORD
UNIVERSITY PRESS

Chip was doing step-ups. He was
training for a football match that
was on the next day.

"Look out!" said Craig. "Your shoelace is undone." But it was too late.

Chip fell onto the bench. He
yelled out in pain. Dad came
running over.

"My leg really hurts," said Chip.
"I can't stand up."

"I think I'd better take you to the
hospital," said Dad.

"Poor Chip," said Dad. "I'll phone
Mum and get her to come and
meet us."

Mum was waiting for them with a wheelchair. "You park the car and I'll check us in. Meet us in the waiting area," she told Dad.

A nurse took Chip and Mum to a
cubicle. "Tell me what happened,"
said the nurse. Chip told him how he
had fallen, and showed him his leg.

"Look at this chart. Point to the
picture to show me how bad the
pain is," said the nurse. "I can give
you some medicine for the pain."

"You need to have an X-ray so we can see if your bone is broken," said the nurse. "The porter will take you for a ride in the wheelchair."

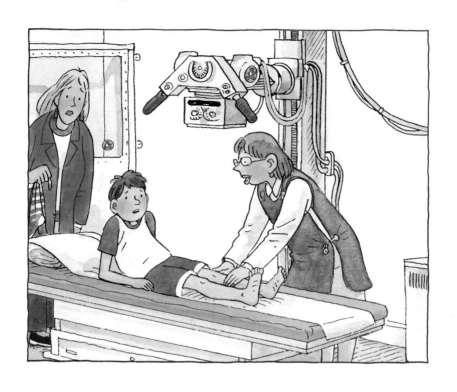

"The X-ray machine takes a picture of the bone in your leg," said the radiographer. "It won't hurt."

"I know," said Chip. "It's OK."

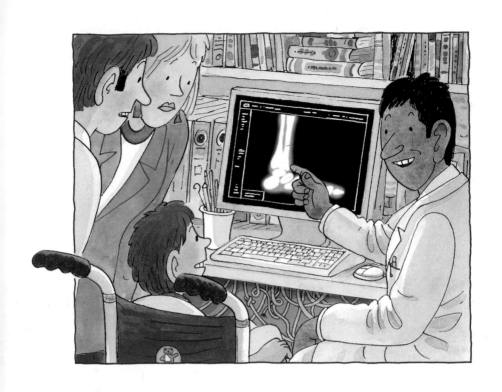

"You've cracked this bone in your leg," said the doctor. "We'll give you a plaster cast now. Then come back on Monday for the fracture clinic."

Mum helped hold Chip's leg while the plaster was put on. "It will feel nice and warm," said the nurse.

"Don't put weight on your leg.
Don't get the plaster wet, or poke
anything down it!" said the nurse.
"If it's sore, tell Mum or Dad."

The nurse gave Chip some crutches
and showed him how to use them.

"It's hard," said Chip.

"You're doing well," said Dad.

The next day, Chip and Craig
watched the football game. "I wish
I was playing," said Chip. "It's so
exciting."

"I play basketball and that's just as exciting," said Craig. "Want to watch me play next week?"

"Yes, please," said Chip.

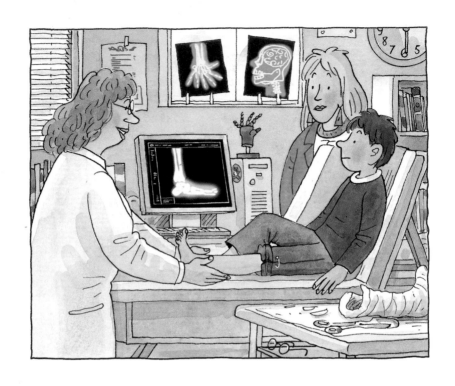

On Monday, Mum took Chip to
the fracture clinic at the hospital.
"The cracked bone will be better
in about six weeks," said the doctor.

Chip got a new cast that he could
walk on. "Can I have a green one?"
he asked. "It's the same colour as
my football team."

Chip showed Biff and Kipper his
new cast. "Can I draw on it?" asked
Kipper.

"No way," said Chip.

"Look out!" said Biff. "Don't trip over Floppy and break your arm too."

The next day, Dad took Chip to
watch Craig play basketball.

"Wow," said Chip. "It's really
exciting. I'd love to play too."

"I'll teach you when your leg is
better," said Craig. "Let's go and
play football now."

"You're really good at this," said
Chip.

"I've had lots of practice!" said
Craig.

Talk about the story

How did Chip hurt his leg?

Why did the radiographer take an x-ray?

How did Chip feel when he was watching the football match?

For what other reasons do children sometimes visit hospital?

If you go to hospital with a broken leg you ...

See a nurse

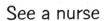

Have an X-ray

Have a plaster cast
put on your leg

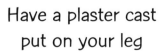

Are given
crutches

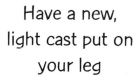

Go back to the
fracture clinic

Have a new,
light cast put on
your leg

What do you think happens
if you break your arm?

Spot the pair

Find the two pictures of Chip that are exactly the same.

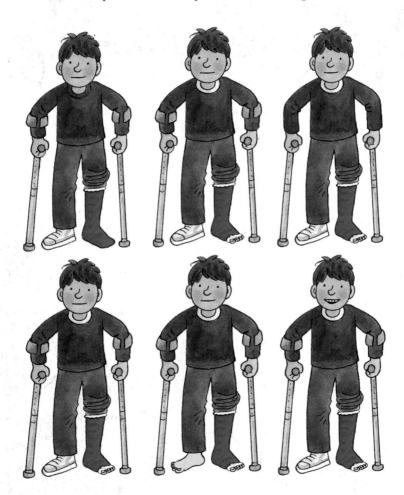